TONGUES:
POWER & BLESSINGS

Secrets of Praying in Tongues revealed.
Increase the power of your prayer-life.
**POWER PRAYER BRINGS
MULTITUDE OF BLESSINGS!**

DONALD LEE

Copyright

Copyright ©2017 by Apostle Donald Lee
www.Godshealingstream.org

All rights reserved. This book or any portion of it may not be reproduced or used in any manner without the written permission of the author except for use of brief quotations in a book review or what is allowed under fair use guidelines.

Notice and Disclaimer: This publication, its author, and publisher expressly disclaim any expressed or implied warranties.

In this book, Donald Lee gives you the best advice he can to help you experience more power and blessings in your life by praying in the Spirit. Outcomes depend on God and His promises in His Word, not Pastor Lee.

Quotations of the Bible in this book are from the public domain. Unless indicated otherwise, all scriptures are from the King James Version (KJV) of the Bible.

Contents

INTRODUCTION 6
1. POWER 8
2. PRAISE 11
3. FAITH 14
4. EDIFYING ONESELF 19
5. COMFORT 23
6. INTERCESSORY HELP 26
7. DELIVERANCE 32
8. HELP FOR THE FUTURE 36
9. GIFTS OF THE SPIRIT 41
10. THE PRESENCE OF GOD 44
11. JOY 52
12. HEARING GOD'S VOICE 58
13. SPEAK GOD'S WILL INTO YOUR LIFE 62
14. COMMANDING TONGUES 67
15. GUIDANCE: LED BY THE SPIRIT 70
16. WORSHIP 73
17. WARFARE 76
18. DISCERNMENT AND TRUTH 79
19. BIRTHING BY THE SPIRIT 82
20. TRUTH VS. MISCONCEPTIONS ABOUT TONGUES 86
21. CONCLUSION 90

FOREWORD

I will never forget the day I opened the package from Pastor Donald Lee. It was Monday morning September 8, 2014 in my home office. Pastor Lee had mailed the package 11 days earlier on August 28, but when it arrived I let it sit on the floor of my office for about a week, thinking "I don't have time to read another book." Little did I realize this simple little book would profoundly change my life and fruitfulness forever and very quickly.

When I opened Pastor Lee's package, inside was his book **Tongues: Power and Blessings**, a companion CD, and a short note that read: "Joseph, Thank you for your masterminding info. Please take a look at this book and let me know if you have any suggestions about a webinar. The CD accompanies the book. Shalom! Donald Lee."

The note inspired me to load the CD in my computer to listen on iTunes. Within five to ten minutes of doing that, Holy Spirit told me I was to read the Tongues book the next morning. When I did, it was as if scales fell off of my eyes. Even though I had a deep and intimate relationship with the Lord, prayed in tongues daily, and was known as a man of prayer, this book opened the eyes of my understanding to realize how powerful praying in tongues is and the many benefits. That motivated me to pray longer and stronger in tongues. And what happened as a result is incredible.

On September 10, the day after reading ***Tongues: Power and Blessings*** for the first time, I was inspired to call Apostle Donald Lee to make him an offer he could not refuse, including joining The Dream Summit and hosting him on a live webinar to share his tongues message with the world. Pastor Lee said yes and made his first financial investment on 9-11. (It's interesting that he lives in New York City near the place where the World Trade Center towers used to be before the 9-11 terrorist attacks.) The next morning we had a private coaching call. Five days after that (September 17), I hosted him on a live professional webinar. The response to his Tongues message was phenomenal, one of the most successful webinars I had ever seen after working seven years hosting live professional webinars.

Since reading ***Tongues: Power and Blessings*** several times, I have experienced enormous growth and blessings personally and professionally. This book is a game changer. I recommend reading it numerous times, including while praying in tongues.

This book is my favorite book on prayer ever and I am an avid reader and man of prayer. I know Apostle Lee very well and can honestly say he is one of the most anointed prayer warriors I have ever met. He lives, breathes, and sleeps praying in tongues. I believe his book, teaching, and impartation will radically transform the Body of Christ globally in these last days to manifest the power of God and prepare the way for the second coming of the Lord. Enjoy!

Blessings to pray longer and pray stronger!

Joseph

Joseph Peck, M.D.
The Time Doctor
Empowering Dreams

INTRODUCTION

THE BAPTISM OF THE HOLY GHOST

What was the very last commandment Jesus gave before He ascended?

"And, behold, I send the promise of my Father upon you: but tarry ye in the city of Jerusalem, until ye be endued with power from on high. And he led them out as far as to Bethany, and he lifted up his hands, and blessed them. And it came to pass, while he blessed them, he was parted from them, and carried up into heaven." (Lk. 24:49-51)

He commanded, not asked, them to wait in Jerusalem until they be filled with power from on high. This experience has come to be known as the baptism of the Holy Ghost. What events occurred when the power from on high fell?

"And when the day of Pentecost was fully come, they were all with one accord in one place. And suddenly there came a sound from heaven as of a rushing mighty wind, and it filled all the house where they were sitting. And there appeared unto them cloven tongues like as of fire, and it sat upon each of them. And they were all filled

with the Holy Ghost, and began to speak with other tongues, as the Spirit gave them utterance." (Acts 2:1-4)

All the disciples spoke with other tongues as the Holy Spirit gave utterance. Now if Jesus instructed the disciples to receive the power from on high, and the speaking in other tongues followed, it is necessary to understand the importance of speaking in tongues. What then are its benefits?

1. POWER

Jesus said that when the Holy Ghost comes upon us we shall have power from on high.

"But ye shall receive power, after that the Holy Ghost is come upon you: and ye shall be witnesses unto me both in Jerusalem, and in all Judaea, and in Samaria, and unto the uttermost part of the earth." (Acts 1:8)

Peter boasted that he would not deny Jesus even if persecution came.

"Peter answered and said unto him, Though all men shall be offended because of thee, yet will I never be offended. Jesus said unto him, Verily I say unto thee, that this night, before the cock crow, thou shalt deny me thrice. Peter said unto him, Though I should die with thee, yet will I not deny thee. Likewise also said all the disciples." (Mat. 26:33-35)

But when the test came, Peter denied Jesus and he denied Him three times. In fact he even cursed and swore to convince them that he was not a disciple (v.75). He did not have the strength to overcome the fear. When Peter realized what he had done, he wept bitterly. You see, Peter meant to stick with Jesus—he wanted to, with all his heart—but he just did not have the power. In the face of the persecution, he just melted away.

On the day of Pentecost, however, it was a different story (Acts 2). When the people started to mock the disciples in the upper room, calling them drunk, Peter stood up and spoke boldly. He didn't run this time. He didn't deny Christ this time. He preached boldly. In fact, so boldly that 3,000 people got saved!

What accounted for the difference in Peter's behavior? It was the Holy Ghost. It was being filled with the Holy Ghost. It was the speaking in tongues. This made Peter a new man. Peter now had power. The situations that had defeated him— the situations that had intimidated him— no longer could overcome him. The Holy Ghost had given him power. He was now endued with power from on high. He now had the power to be courageous.

We can have the same power as Peter had. When we receive the baptism of the Holy Spirit, when we speak in tongues fervently, we will be filled with the Holy Ghost, and the Holy Ghost will give us power. The Holy Ghost will transform us. The Holy Ghost will transform us from grasshoppers to giants in the Spirit.

REVIEW & EXERCISE

Chapter 1:

Q1: What was your life like before and after you received the baptism of the Holy Ghost?

Q2: What fruit have you produced with the Holy Ghost that you could not have without Him?

Exercise: Try to accomplish something you have never done while praying and asking the Holy Ghost for help.

2. PRAISE

"Who can utter the mighty acts of the LORD? Who can shew forth all his praise?" (Ps. 106:2)

This scripture asks who is able to give forth all the praise that God deserves. This verse challenges us to try to do so. If we think about this, we will see that it is not so easy. We might be able to quickly rattle off some of the mighty acts of the Lord, but then we will slow up, scratch our heads, and struggle to recall some of the others.

God presents a tough challenge to us. Seems impossible for us to fulfill. But God also supplies the solution. What is the solution? Speaking in tongues! When we speak in tongues we allow the Holy Ghost to praise God through our lips. How do we know that the Spirit is praising God in tongues? Look at Acts 2:1-11.

"Cretes and Arabians, we do hear them speak in our tongues the wonderful works of God." (Acts 2:11)

On the day of Pentecost there were merchants from all over the world in Jerusalem. When the Holy Ghost fell in the upper room, these foreigners on the street heard the Jewish disciples praising the wonderful works of God in their native languages. People from Arabia, for example, heard some of the disciples praising God in the Arabic language. So in those tongues we allow the Holy Ghost to praise God. As we do this, something unusual happens. These tongues of praise start rolling out of our lips so effortlessly. We do not need to use our brains to do any thinking. And at the same time, our soul feels so fulfilled.

This is the beauty of praising the Lord in tongues. We can go on and on, non-stop, praising God in this way. The Holy Ghost in us, through those tongues, can utter forth all the praise that God deserves!

REVIEW & EXERCISE

Chapter 2:

Q1: What do you do when you have prayed all you know how to pray for?

Q2: What is the easiest form of prayer that we can do without even thinking about it?

Exercise: Try to pray for an hour without interruption.

3. FAITH

"But ye, beloved, building up yourselves on your most holy faith, praying in the Holy Ghost."
(Jude 20)

Praying in the Holy Ghost is praying in tongues. Jude 20 is telling us that our faith increases as we pray in tongues. When we pray in tongues, the Holy Ghost downloads impressions and messages from the Spirit-realm into our inner man. For the common carnal human being, what he believes in is based on what his five senses feed him, so it is hard for him to believe in spiritual things. But when we become born-again and Spirit-filled and pray much in tongues, our inner man starts to be filled with spiritual impressions from the Holy Ghost. So our thinking and belief system is now more and more influenced by the impressions from the Holy Ghost and true faith can now arise.

Now the more filled we are with information from the natural world, the harder it is to have that faith which pleases God. To increase in faith we need to be filled more and more with information from the heavenly world. When Peter was walking on the water and he looked around, he was thinking, *"Winds, waves, rough waters. Nature is stronger than man. The force* *of gravity is greater than man."* He was not thinking, "The Lord Jesus is the Creator. The Creator is greater than creation. When the Creator speaks creation must obey." And so he began to sink.

When we pray in tongues, however, we are allowing the Holy Ghost to speak things about God's nature and God's laws into our inner man. Now the intellect does not understand these words of the Holy Ghost, but it does not matter. The inner man can receive things and understand things even when the natural mind does not have the understanding. How many times have we gotten the feeling that a person we have just met is not good, even though we have not really talked to him or know anything about him? We may call this an intuition and then later we find out that this person was not a good person. This shows that the inner man can understand things even when the intellect has not.

One time, in the building that we were renting for our church services, one of the steps on the staircase was cracked. I called the landlord, and he said he would send over the carpenter to look at it. When the carpenter came over to look at it, however, he smirked and said that it was such a little job that we, the tenants, should take care of it ourselves. And then in a huff he walked off. That evening we had a prayer meeting, but I was so worried about the cracked step I could not pray. I kept thinking, "*The landlord will refuse to fix it because of the nasty carpenter. The carpenter does not want to fix it. He's going to tell the landlord 'Don't fix it', that it's so minor that the tenants can fix it themselves. The step is not going to be fixed because the carpenter doesn't want to fix it.*" Then I imagined someone falling and getting injured and suing the church for a million dollars. I kept worrying about this for a long, long time.

Finally I was able to start praying in tongues. As I prayed in tongues I noticed that I kept repeating over and over again one particular sentence in tongues. This went on for about 45 minutes or so. At this point my fears were beginning to die down. Then suddenly the Holy Ghost revealed to me what I was saying in tongues: *"God is sovereign."* With that, all my fears completely ceased. My faith sprang up. I believed that somehow the step was going to be fixed because God was still in charge.

Well, late that evening, when I got home, the carpenter called. "When are you going to be at the church so I can come over and fix the step?" he asked. Hallelujah! You see, the Spirit was declaring that God is sovereign. He is the final authority. It doesn't matter what man says. Even if man says he does not want to do something God can make him do it!

From this experience I learned that the Holy Ghost in those tongues many times speaks to us a message, or a truth about God, or even a scripture. The Holy Ghost plants it deep into our inner man; and as He repeats this message, our inner man receives it and faith is built up.

REVIEW & EXERCISE

Chapter 3:

Q1: What is the difference between praying in the Holy Ghost and praying in tongues?

Q2: How do you pray the perfect prayer?

Exercise: Try to pray in tongues without asking God for anything.

4. EDIFYING ONESELF

"He that speaketh in an unknown tongue edifieth himself; but he that prophesieth edifieth the church." (1 Cor. 14:4)

To edify means to build up. So when we pray in tongues we build ourselves up. **We do not have to be downcast**, discouraged or left feeling small. If we would pray in tongues the Holy Ghost will build us up. God never intended for us to be down low. This is not humility—this is being defeated! We are supposed to be overcomers (1 Jn. 4:4; Rev. 12:11). Our heads should be held up high. God's purpose for us is to have our heads up high.

"But thou, O LORD, art a shield for me; my glory, and the lifter up of mine head." (Ps 3:3)

God is the Most High God, not a low god (Gen. 14:22; Ps. 78:56) The Holy Ghost is the Spirit of the Highest (Lk. 1:35). God does not make weak, groveling Christians. If they would only pray in tongues they would not have to be that way. God's will is to take us up, set us up on high (Ps. 91:14). The Holy Ghost will build us up. He will edify us. However, sometimes we may have to pray more than short little three-minute prayers to be edified.

When I first got saved, right from the onset of my Christian walk I experienced grave difficulties. But through the difficulties I learned of the power of speaking in tongues. When I was just a baby Christian, someone who called herself a Christian almost killed me in a fit of rage. I narrowly escaped with my life. But for weeks afterwards I was walking around in a state of shock. I could not believe that it had happened to me. I condemned and blamed myself for allowing it to have happened to me. In fact, I was tormented with guilt. Then I began to think that I had lost my salvation. I had hit rock bottom...and to think, I had just gotten saved a little while before that.

Well, anyway, after several weeks I had an idea. I thought I would try to pray in tongues. I figured that if I could pray in tongues again then I must still be saved. So I started to pray, and I was able to even pray in tongues again. But after a few days, every time that I prayed in tongues I would start thinking that those were not God's tongues, but the devil's tongues! So I really was not filled with the Holy Ghost anymore. And if I was not filled with the Holy Ghost anymore, I probably was not saved anymore either. So for days and days I battled these thoughts. Nevertheless, I just kept praying in those tongues. Whether they were God's or the devil's, I had no choice; there was nothing else I could think of doing.

Day after day I prayed in tongues, from 45 minutes up to an hour or more. Then I began to notice that these doubts and negative thoughts started to decrease. The tormenting idea that I was speaking the devil's tongues began to cease. I started to get confidence in myself again... *"Maybe I was still saved,"* I figured. Then some days later, it was *"I know I'm saved. Jesus forgives even the stupidest of mistakes."* And my spirit started to pick up again. Soon I was looking up, and back "on my feet" again. Yes, I can testify from personal experience that praying in tongues will edify you, even if you have hit rock bottom!

REVIEW & EXERCISE

Chapter 4:

Q1: How do we build ourselves up in the holy faith?

Q2: How long do we pray in tongues while trying to have victory over an obstacle?

Exercise: Pray in tongues longer than you normally do for a smaller victory.

5. COMFORT

Along with the edifying power of the Holy Ghost, the Holy Ghost can function as the Comforter, giving us much needed comfort in our low seasons. Over and over again Jesus called the Holy Ghost the Comforter. Get to know the Holy Ghost as the Sweet Comforter!

"But the Comforter, which is the Holy Ghost, whom the Father will send in my name, he shall teach you all things, and bring all things to your remembrance, whatsoever I have said unto you." (Jn. 14:26)

"But when the Comforter is come, whom I will send unto you from the Father, even the Spirit of truth, which proceedeth from the Father, he shall testify of me." (Jn. 15:26)

"Nevertheless I tell you the truth; It is expedient for you that I go away: for if I go not away, the Comforter will not come unto you; but if I depart, I will send him unto you." (Jn. 16:7)

Indeed the Holy Ghost will function as a Comforter to us when we pray much in the Spirit. When I first began to pastor, I became discouraged by some mistakes I was making and got so discouraged I did not want to preach anymore. I felt very low and not qualified to edify the people when I wasn't edified myself.

But I learned the power of praying in tongues. As I forced myself to pray in the Spirit, regardless of how low I felt, I began to "pick up steam." After an hour or so I was 'up' again. I felt the comfort of the Holy Ghost deep down in my soul. There was such a sweet feeling inside me.

"O taste and see that the LORD is good: blessed is the man that trusteth in him." (Ps. 34:8)

If the saints would understand that the Holy Ghost can be a Comforter, the spirit of discouragement would not have so much power against the church of God. The Holy Ghost as Comforter pours the love of God into our hearts as the antidote against discouragement. Hallelujah! We never need to be defeated! Victory is always within our grasp through the power of praying in the Spirit!

"And hope maketh not ashamed; because the love of God is shed abroad in our hearts by the Holy Ghost which is given unto us." (Rom. 5:5)

But one important point to emphasize: Many times the comfort does not come just as soon as you start praying in the Spirit. You may have to pray for long periods of time, as God often will test our commitment and resolve. In getting to experience the comfort of the Holy Ghost sometimes I had to pray in tongues for two hours or more. So learn to be patient.

REVIEW & EXERCISE

Chapter 5:

Q1: Why did Jesus leave us for the Holy Ghost to come?

Q2: What are the benefits of the Holy Ghost?

Exercise: Ask the Holy Ghost to show you someone who needs comforted and go encourage him or her.

6. INTERCESSORY HELP

"The heart is deceitful above all things, and desperately wicked: who can know it?" (Jer. 17:9)

"Likewise the Spirit also helpeth our infirmities: for we know not what we should pray for as we ought: but the Spirit itself maketh intercession for us with groanings which cannot be uttered. 27And he that searcheth the hearts knoweth what is the mind of the Spirit, because he maketh intercession for the saints according to the will of God." (Rom. 8:26-27)

Romans 8:26 states that we do not know how to pray as we should. And when it comes to praying for ourselves this is especially true. Why is that? Because the heart is deceitful (Jer. 17.9). We lie to ourselves and suppress feelings and deny them. Deep within our hearts there may fester layers of resentment, bitterness, unforgiveness, anger, etc. But we will deny that these things exist in us because we are so 'spiritual.' And because these things exist and remain within us, our spiritual growth is hindered. They remain lodged inside because we do not want to recognize their existence and therefore, we do not pray for God to take them out.

Many Christians get stuck in their spiritual growth for a long time. It's because they will pray for everything except for those things that are really affecting their soul. They go around in circles wandering around the same mountain like the children of Israel.

But thank God for the Holy Ghost. When we pray fervently in tongues the Holy Ghost can intercede for us. He helps us in our infirmities (emotional weaknesses) by making intercession for us. The Bible says that the Lord knows what we need.

"Be not ye therefore like unto them: for your Father knoweth what things ye have need of, before ye ask him." (Mat. 6:8)

"(For after all these things do the Gentiles seek:) for your heavenly Father knoweth that ye have need of all these things." (Mat. 6:32)

God knows all the "junk" on the inside that we need to get rid of. And He can do those things that we have need of even before we ask Him in our natural language—that is, even before we become aware of these unpleasant things and before we muster enough courage to admit them and call on Him to pull them out. How is it possible to get things from the Lord before we even ask Him? Because the Holy Ghost has already asked the Father in that spiritual language! This is one of the secrets to getting strong in the Lord. The more we speak in tongues the more quickly Jesus can pull out those weaknesses.

I discovered this one time when I was praying in the Spirit for a good length of time. Suddenly I began to feel a little sad. Then I actually started to weep. What then came to my mind was something I had done to someone. At the time that the action occurred I did not feel it was wrong. But now in my prayer time I could see that it was definitely wrong. And at this point I repented before God. From this experience I understood that the Holy Ghost was bringing up my behavior. At the same time the Holy Ghost was sending a spirit of conviction into my heart. The Holy Ghost was putting the incident into my mind, showing me my wrong, and then causing me to repent. With my natural mind and natural speech, I would never have had the honesty or courage to admit to God that I had been wrong. But thank God for the Holy Ghost. He can do these wonderful things for us without our even being aware when it is happening!

"For we know not what we should pray for as we ought." Because we do not know how to pray as we ought to, many times we are disappointed that God has not answered and given us what we asked for. But what we asked for may not be in God's perfect will. For example, I might pray this way: "Lord Jesus, give me that beautiful

new car I saw today." But then if I pray in tongues the Holy Ghost might be saying, "Oh God, give him that used car that he needs."

You see, God is wiser than we are. He knows that if I got that brand new car, I might get caught up in pampering it, getting all upset over every nick and scratch on it, that it might become an idol to me and pull me away from God.

The more we speak in tongues the more we can have our needs met and get those things that we spiritually need! Those who pray more will get more from the Lord. Once I met a Christian who claimed that Romans 8:26 had nothing to do with praying in tongues. But I told him to go on to verse 27, and not just take verse 26 out of context. *"He that searcheth"* in verse 27 refers to God the Father. *"Knows what is the mind of the Spirit"* means that God understands the mind of the Spirit; that something must have been done or said which is not readily understood, but that God understands what the Spirit is trying to communicate because God knows the mind of the Spirit. The *"groanings which cannot be uttered"* of verse 26 are the utterances which we human beings would not speak in our normal everyday language. These groanings and words in tongues are not understandable to us, but understandable to God, because He knows the mind of the Spirit. And God is able to understand easily what the Spirit is doing because the Spirit is merely doing what is the will of God anyway.

REVIEW & EXERCISE

Chapter 6:

Q1: Why do so many prayers go unanswered?

Q2: Why does God give sometimes what we want and other times not?

Exercise: Try praying for God's will and not your own this time and see what happens?

7. DELIVERANCE

Although we may be saved, and have repented of our sins, we still may have some "hang-ups" (inner emotional problems), which may take a bit of time for us to shed. **The shedding of these unpleasant personality traits is known as sanctification or deliverance.** This is not an overnight process! As the angel sent by God brought the burning coal of fire to purge the mouth of Isaiah from the habit of saying ungodly things (Isa. 6:7-8), so the fire of the Holy Ghost can purify us of our faults and weaknesses. As we pray fervently in tongues the Holy Ghost and His fire is stirred up to work for us and to transform our personalities!

Suppose you had very demanding parents. Their standards were very high. No matter what you did they wanted you to do it better and faster. So as a child you internalize these qualities. You become very impatient and demanding, with yourself and with others. When you grow up you become a Christian. Now, as a Christian, you are saved, but you still have this impatient spirit. You as a Christian need deliverance from this impatient spirit. How will you get it?

Praying in the Spirit is one way to get the deliverance, because the Holy Spirit is a sanctifier.

". . . because God hath from the beginning chosen you to salvation through sanctification of the Spirit and belief of the truth." (2 The. 2:13)

"Elect according to the foreknowledge of God the Father, through sanctification of the Spirit, unto obedience and sprinkling of the blood of Jesus Christ . . ." (1 Pet. 1:2)

"That I should be the minister of Jesus Christ to the Gentiles, ministering the gospel of God, that the offering up of the Gentiles might be acceptable, being sanctified by the Holy Ghost." (Rom. 15:16)

The emotional problem that you need deliverance from may seem like a solid rock that has been with you and plagued you from childhood, but as you pray in tongues consistently and fervently, the Holy Ghost chips away at it little by little. Layer by layer, like an onion, the Holy Ghost peels away that yoke.

The Holy Ghost is likened unto a fire, and in this form He can surely purge us of our faults:

"When the LORD shall have washed away the filth of the daughters of Zion, and shall have purged the blood of Jerusalem from the midst thereof by the spirit of judgment, and by the spirit of burning." (Isa. 4:4)

The purging of the people in Isaiah 4:4 takes place by the spirit of burning. Many times as we pray in tongues we feel the fire of the Spirit. As a fire He can accomplish many things at the same time, one of them being deliverance. Many people object to praying in tongues because they do not understand what they are saying. But if we did understand we might give God a hard time. When the Holy Ghost is bringing up our faults we would tell God, *"It's not true what the Holy Ghost is saying about me. I'm not like that."* So thank God we do not understand the tongues; then the Holy Ghost can make the intercession for us uninterrupted. Notice that the Holy Ghost is making intercession for us, because of our weaknesses, and at the same time He is the agent of the deliverance from these weaknesses.

By the way, **praying in tongues in private needs no interpretation**. The speaking in tongues in a public setting that leads to prophecy is the kind of tongues that needs interpretation (more about that later).

REVIEW & EXERCISE

Chapter 7:

Q1: When we become born-again, are we completely set free from the bondages that hold us back?

Q2: How do we pray without being able to see what only God can reveal?

Exercise: Pray in tongues and ask the Holy Ghost to reveal a stumbling block in your life that you may not see.

8. HELP FOR THE FUTURE

We do not know what dangers and what temptations lurk ahead in the future for us, so naturally we cannot really pray effectively for future events; but the Holy Ghost, which is the Spirit of Jesus, knows everything—past, present, and future! So when we pray in tongues we are allowing the Holy Spirit to intercede for us to the Father regarding future problems that may arise.

God is a God who goes ahead of His people to prepare the defeat of the enemy:

"Understand therefore this day, that the LORD thy God is he which goeth over before thee; as a consuming fire he shall destroy them, and he shall bring them down before thy face: so shalt thou drive them out, and destroy them quickly, as the LORD hath said unto thee." (Deu. 9:3)

"The LORD thy God, he will go over before thee, and he will destroy these nations from before thee, and thou shalt possess them: and Joshua, he shall go over before thee, as the LORD hath said." (Deu. 31:3)

As the children of Israel approached Jericho, God went before His people into Jericho and put fear into the hearts of the inhabitants there. Before the Israelites even got to Jericho, the heathen's hearts had already melted. They were as good as dead already, even before the battle had actually begun. So when the actual war started, it was very easy for the children of Israel to get the victory.

"And she said unto the men, I know that the LORD hath given you the land, and that your terror is fallen upon us, and that all the inhabitants of the land faint because of you. For we have heard how the LORD dried up the water of the Red sea for you, when ye came out of Egypt; and what ye did unto the two kings of the Amorites, that were on the other side Jordan, Sihon and Og, whom ye utterly destroyed. And as soon as we had heard these things, our hearts did melt, neither did there remain any more courage in any man, because of you: for the LORD your God, he is God in heaven above, and in earth beneath." (Jos. 2:9-11)

Likewise, the Holy Ghost, through the intercession in tongues, goes ahead to prepare victory for us. Because He already knows what lies ahead for us, the Holy Ghost can petition God to give us what we need when that future crisis arrives, so that when we do meet that problem we can conquer it and be victorious! Many Christians are "Crisis Christians"—they only get into serious prayer when they are in a serious crisis. Then they have to sweat it out, living dangerously, on the brink of disaster. But why wait for the potential disaster to come upon you before you pray seriously (and in a panic, I may add)? If we do much praying in tongues now, those future things may not have a chance to mushroom into a crisis. The praying in tongues nullifies many future dangers.

So praying in tongues in the present time assures victories in the future!

One time, while I was still working as a school teacher, I prayed in tongues in the morning longer than my customary amount of time. It was the Holy Ghost that had me praying that way. When I finally got to school, for some reason I just felt like going up to my room using a different staircase from my usual one. In the mid-morning, about two hours after class had started a parent entered into my room. The first thing he asked me was where I had been. He explained to me that he had planned to meet me downstairs and take care of a matter with me concerning his son. The principal had told him which stairs I usually take to get to my room. So the parent went there hoping to meet me. He waited two hours there (not knowing I came up another way) before deciding to come up to see if I was already in my room.

Next, he asked me in a hostile way why I had hit his son the day before. I told him that was an absolute lie. As I told him what really happened with his son, the father calmed down and saw that his son had been lying. The father then smiled, shook my hand, and then went on to confess to me that he had planned to "straighten me out" that morning. He was going to shout me down for what he had believed I had done to his son, and even hit me. As he was talking, I realized the intercessory help the Holy Ghost had given me. It was the Holy Ghost that made me go up another staircase, causing that parent to wait there for two hours, which cooled his temper down enough so that he was able to listen to reason! If I had not prayed in tongues extra that morning I might have had a couple of teeth knocked out of my mouth by some irate parent.

He who prays much in tongues today decreases the problems of tomorrow.

REVIEW & EXERCISE

Chapter 8:

Q1: Do you consider yourself a "Crisis Christian?"

Q2: What events in your life were avoided by simply praying in tongues beforehand?

Exercise: Pray in tongues for at least ten minutes before you start your day.

9. GIFTS OF THE SPIRIT

The gifts of the Spirit (1 Cor. 12), such as the gift of prophecy and the gift of healing, come from the Spirit. In other words, the Holy Spirit brings the gifts, but it is by dwelling much in the Spirit that we can obtain these gifts. Paul was the mightiest apostle. One of the keys to his power in Christ was that he prayed in tongues more than any of the other disciples around (1 Cor. 14:18).

So if you want the gifts of the Spirit to operate in your life, pray much in tongues. If you want the Holy Ghost to operate His gifts in your life, you must make Him welcome in your temple. You do this by letting Him express Himself by praying much in tongues. As you let Him become more and more dominant in your life He will then begin to operate those gifts.

When I first received the Holy Ghost, I would pray much in tongues in my house. I would pray in tongues in one room until I got tired. Then I would get up and walk around a bit, and then go to another room to continue praying in tongues. In this way, I went from room to room praying in tongues. Several months later, I noticed that I was getting warm sensations in the palm of my hands. And as the days went on, the more I prayed in tongues the warmer the palm of my hand got. Then one day I met someone who was not feeling well. I laid my hands on him, and, lo and behold, immediately the person got better! At that point, I realized that I had the gift of healing.

In a like manner the gift of prophecy also got stirred up in me when I prayed much in tongues. One time a lady asked me to pray for her. At that point in time I was a newly ordained minister, but I had not operated in the gift of prophecy. As she stood before me I prayed for what I felt were her needs. Then I went into tongues. As I was praying in tongues I heard in my spirit the word *'heart.'* As I kept praying in tongues this word got stronger and stronger. Finally I just blurted out without any premeditation, *"There's a heart problem."* The lady quickly nodded her head and said she had a weak heart and was on medication. So at that point I prayed for her heart, and the presence of God came on her and she felt much stronger.

As time went on I added to the practice of praying in tongues regular fasting, sometimes even going on long fasts. The result was that the gifts of the Spirit got stronger.

REVIEW & EXERCISE

Chapter 9:

Q1: Why was Paul one of the most effective Apostles in the Bible?

Q2: What separates us from walking in what Apostle Paul walked in?

Exercise: If you desire one of the gifts of the Spirit, pray in tongues until it manifests in your life.

10. THE PRESENCE OF GOD

"Even the Spirit of truth; whom the world cannot receive, because it seeth him not, neither knoweth him: but ye know him; for he dwelleth with you, and shall be in you." (Jn. 14:17)

"Behold, a virgin shall be with child, and shall bring forth a son, and they shall call his name Emmanuel, which being interpreted is, God with us." (Matt. 1:23)

"To whom God would make known what is the riches of the glory of this mystery among the Gentiles; which is Christ in you, the hope of glory." (Col. 1:27)

When Christ walked the earth He was Emmanuel, which is God with us. But now, through His Holy Spirit, He can be to us God in us! In John 14:17, Jesus foretold of the time when the Spirit, instead of just being with the believers, would be in them. When the believer is baptized in the Holy Ghost he now has the Holy Ghost in him, and he can be filled with the Spirit, or filled with the presence of the Lord.

God never intended to be a faraway God. That is why He had Moses build the tabernacle—so that God could now dwell among mankind.

"And let them make me a sanctuary; that I may dwell among them." (Exo. 25:8)

And that's why He says to draw near to Him and He will draw near to us.

"Draw nigh to God, and he will draw nigh to you. Cleanse your hands, ye sinners; and purify your hearts, ye double minded." (Jas. 4:8)

He wants to be close to us; yea, He wants to be in us. And if this is true, which it is, then we should be able to feel His presence. Yes, the Lord wants to be felt. And we can all have heart-felt experiences of the presence of the Lord just as the two disciples of Emmaus had.

"And they said one to another, Did not our heart burn within us, while he talked with us by the way, and while he opened to us the scriptures?" (Lk. 24:32)

While Jesus fellowshipped with them, their hearts burned within them. Jesus was not only fellowshipping with them on the outside, but He was also fellowshipping within them. He was giving them a preview of the time when the disciples after being baptized with the Spirit would be able to feel the fire of his presence within them. Yes, all the disciples of the Lord can feel the fire of His presence within them when they receive His Spirit and learn to be filled with the Spirit. Psalm 22:3 tells us that God lives within the praises of His people:

"But thou art holy, O thou that inhabitest the praises of Israel." (Ps. 22:3)

When we come into the presence of the Lord with a heart of devotion and praise, and open our mouth and praise him in the Spirit, God will dwell within that praise. Yes, praising God in tongues will bring the presence of God into us. There is no reason any Christians should be dry and weary, and not feel Jesus within himself. God never intended it to this way.

Just being baptized with the Holy Ghost, however, does not guarantee that we will feel His presence. We must live a life of praising the Lord in the Spirit. When I first got the Holy Ghost I felt the presence of the Lord in a fiery way, as many others have experienced. That initial experience of being baptized in the Spirit was so wonderful. But soon it became a distant memory, and I started to become dry. Then I heard a sermon in which the preacher said that if we were not experiencing consistently the fiery presence of God, then we needed to praise the Lord much more fervently.

So I learned that I had to praise Him much more than just a few moments on Sundays. **I had to learn to praise Him regardless of what my emotions felt like doing. I had to learn to**

praise him even if my body did not want to.
And so I had to learn to make praising God in the Spirit a way of life. So I made up my mind to start praising Him more in the Spirit. At first, I did not immediately feel the presence of God come on me. But as time went on, over the course of the next weeks and months, I began to feel the presence of the Lord growing on me. At first, I was so dry that it took an effort on my part to even lift my hands and give the Lord a wave-praise. But as time went on it became more effortless, and then it began to happen spontaneously. I found that the fire of His presence was increasing so much that sometimes I couldn't contain myself. I couldn't sit still in the pews. I had to get up and wave my hands or do something with my body to praise him. Yes, we can actually feel God in our body.

Look at the Major Prophets. They all experienced the presence of God.

"In the year that king Uzziah died I saw also the LORD sitting upon a throne, high and lifted up, and his train filled the temple. Above it stood the seraphims: each one had six wings; with twain he covered his face, and with twain he covered his feet, and with twain he did fly. And one cried unto another, and said, Holy, holy, holy, is the LORD of hosts: the whole earth is full of his glory. And the posts of the door moved at the voice of him that cried, and the house was

filled with smoke. Then said I, Woe is me! for I am undone; because I am a man of unclean lips, and I dwell in the midst of a people of unclean lips: for mine eyes have seen the King, the LORD of hosts. Then flew one of the seraphims unto me, having a live coal in his hand, which he had taken with the tongs from off the altar: And he laid it upon my mouth, and said, Lo, this hath touched thy lips; and thine iniquity is taken away, and thy sin purged. Also I heard the voice of the LORD, saying, Whom shall I send, and who will go for us? Then said I, Here am I; send me." (Isa. 6:1-8)

Isaiah saw, heard and felt God. With his eyes he saw the glory of God. With his ears he heard the audible voice of God. And with his mouth he tasted the sanctification power of God.

Jeremiah felt the presence of God in his bones.

"Then I said, I will not make mention of him, nor speak any more in his name. But his word was in mine heart as a burning fire shut up in my bones, and I was weary with forbearing, and I could not stay." (Jer. 20:9)

Ezekiel experienced God picking him up, and even tasted God as God manifested as the Word.

"And he said unto me, Son of man, stand upon thy feet, and I will speak unto thee. And the spirit entered into me when he spake unto me,

and set me upon my feet, that I heard him that spake unto me." (Ezk. 2:1-2)

"Moreover he said unto me, Son of man, eat that thou findest; eat this roll, and go speak unto the house of Israel. So I opened my mouth, and he caused me to eat that roll. And he said unto me, Son of man, cause thy belly to eat, and fill thy bowels with this roll that I give thee. Then did I eat it; and it was in my mouth as honey for sweetness." (Ezk. 3:1-3)

"And it came to pass in the sixth year, in the sixth month, in the fifth day of the month, as I sat in mine house, and the elders of Judah sat before me, that the hand of the LORD GOD fell there upon me. Then I beheld, and lo a likeness as the appearance of fire: from the appearance of his loins even downward, fire; and from his loins even upward, as the appearance of brightness, as the colour of amber. And he put forth the form of an hand, and took me by a lock of mine head; and the spirit lifted me up between the earth and the heaven, and brought me in the visions of God to Jerusalem, to the door of the inner gate that looketh toward the north; where was the seat of the image of jealousy, which provoketh to jealousy." (Ezk. 8:1-3)

In the New Testament, we see two disciples experiencing Jesus in the midst of their hearts.

"And they said one to another, Did not our heart burn within us, while he talked with us by the way, and while he opened to us the scriptures?" (Lk. 24:32)

In this dispensation, the Holy Ghost is the person of the Godhead through whom we can experience the presence of God the most. The Holy Ghost likes to be invited into our midst. Jesus entered the house of the disciples of Emmaus only after they constrained Him to stay with them.

"And they drew nigh unto the village, whither they went: and he made as though he would have gone further. But they constrained him, saying, Abide with us: for it is toward evening, and the day is far spent. And he went in to tarry with them." (Lk. 24:28-29)

The Holy Ghost feels welcome when we allow Him to have His way in our lives. Praying in the Holy Ghost is the most common way of inviting Him to be present with us.

One reason why many young people do not want to come to church is because they have only experienced dry, boring church services. They want to feel something. They want to experience something with their bodies and souls. We need to introduce them to the God that can be felt in their bodies and experienced in their souls.

REVIEW & EXERCISE

Chapter 10:

Q1: Are we able to sing in tongues?

Q2: What's the difference between praying in tongues and praising in tongues?

Exercise: Try to praise God in tongues, like you would during worship.

11. JOY

On the day of Pentecost, as the Holy Ghost was poured out on the disciples, they started to act like they were drunk. **Being filled with the Spirit caused them to be ecstatic.** This was not some inner intellectual joy. The joy was both inner and outer, deep and plainly visible.

"Others mocking, said, These men are full of new wine." (Acts 2:13)

The people down on the street, looking up at the upper room could see that the disciples were acting drunk. If the people down on the street could see this, then it means that the disciples were really acting demonstratively. They were thoroughly exuberant.

Paul exhorted the church to be filled with the Holy Ghost, and not be drunk with wine.

"And be not drunk with wine, wherein is excess; but be filled with the Spirit." (Eph. 5:18)

He said this because there is an ecstasy that came with being filled with the Spirit. So there were two kinds of intoxications: one from the Spirit and one from alcohol. Paul was saying to choose the one that comes from the Spirit that is of much more benefit than the one that comes from being drunk with wine. As we pray in tongues more and more, the Holy Ghost fills our soul with increasing quantities of these living waters. The joy bubbles up and we start to overflow with this divine ecstasy.

Joy is of God. Jesus did not die on the cross to raise up a church of sad-sack Christians. Jesus wants us to have joy.

"These things have I spoken unto you, that my joy might remain in you, and that your joy might be full." (Jn. 15:11)

"Hitherto have ye asked nothing in my name: ask, and ye shall receive, that your joy may be full." (Jn. 16:24)

"And now come I to thee; and these things I speak in the world, that they might have my joy fulfilled in themselves." (Jn. 17:13)

God is happy. God laughs. So if we are His children, children destined for eternal life, we should be happy, too. We should be people of laughter. When the Holy Ghost is poured out on us, many times we will experience exuberant joy, and even laughter. Sometimes there is even uncontrolled laughter that we cannot stop. These outpourings of joy also break yokes of depression, self-pity, sorrow and pessimism.

"He that sitteth in the heavens shall laugh: the LORD shall have them in derision." (Ps. 2:4)

The Holy Ghost is the one who gives us this joy now:

"And the disciples were filled with joy, and with the Holy Ghost." (Acts 13:52)

"For the kingdom of God is not meat and drink; but righteousness, and peace, and joy in the Holy Ghost." (Rom. 14:17)

***"But the fruit of the Spirit is love, joy,** peace, longsuffering, gentleness, goodness, faith." (Gal. 5:22)*

The Holy Ghost desires to bring us into the presence of God.

"For through him we both have access by one Spirit unto the Father." (Eph. 2:18)

As we pray in tongues we are allowing the Holy Ghost to have His way. His desire is to bring us into the presence of God. When we come into God's presence, what happens?

"Thou wilt shew me the path of life: in thy presence is fullness of joy; at thy right hand there are pleasures for evermore." (Ps. 16:11)

Psalms 16:11 not only tells us that we receive joy in the presence of God, but it is fullness of joy! Just like on the day of Pentecost. Being filled with joy is part of our inheritance as Christians. It is ours. We are supposed to have it. For someone to try to talk us out of it is unscriptural.

There are many reasons the Lord wants us to have joy. The joy of the Lord is our strength. Joy gives us strength. It will help turn a weak Christ into a strong one. Joy and the expression of it physically give glory to God. Joy will make the sinners jealous of what we Christians have and draw many of them to the Lord. Some people will criticize you if you express too much joy, claiming that you are being emotional—dwelling in the realm of the soul and not the Spirit. Well, God gave us a body, soul, and spirit. And all are supposed to be used for God's glory.

"Then he said unto them, Go your way, eat the fat, and drink the sweet, and send portions unto them for whom nothing is prepared: for this day is holy unto our LORD: neither be ye sorry; for the joy of the LORD is your strength." (Neh. 8:10)

"For ye are bought with a price: therefore glorify God in your body, and in your spirit, which are God's." (1 Cor. 6:20)

Now, for those who pray much in tongues you may notice things beginning to happen in your emotions and in your body. You may experience the feeling that you want to "let loose" with your body. You may feel the urge to break out into a shout of joy, or you may want to pop up and break into a Holy Ghost dance. As the joy begins to come on your body just let it flow. Express it with your whole body. Don't quench it. As you flow with it, it will increase.

"Quench not the Spirit." (1 The. 5:19)

If you have not experienced these things yet, keep on praying much in tongues day after day, sooner or later you will experience this deep joy.

We are supposed to make the world jealous of us, of what we have. If we do not manifest joy, why would the people of the world want to be saved? Salvation would have nothing to offer them. We have to show the world that in Christ we have something the world can't buy. **We have what the world wants: Deep Joy.**

REVIEW & EXERCISE

Chapter 11:

Q1: What's being "drunk with new wine" mean?

Q2: When we come into God's presence, what happens?

Exercise: While praying in tongues, ask the Holy Ghost to fill you with joy!

12. HEARING GOD'S VOICE

The Good Shepherd speaks to His sheep, and the sheep hear His voice and recognize His voice.

"To him the porter openeth; and the sheep hear his voice: and he calleth his own sheep by name, and leadeth them out. 4And when he putteth forth his own sheep, he goeth before them, and the sheep follow him: for they know his voice." (Jn. 10:3-4)

"And other sheep I have, which are not of this fold: them also I must bring, and they shall hear my voice; and there shall be one fold, and one shepherd." (Jn. 10:16)

"My sheep hear my voice*, and I know them, and they follow me." (Jn. 10:27)*

Jesus Christ the Good Shepherd wants to speak to His sheep. In this dispensation, **He speaks to His sheep through His Spirit, the Holy Spirit!**

Praying much in tongues is one way to develop an ear to hear the voice of the Lord. When we pray much in tongues we are allowing the Holy Ghost to speak through us. As we do this more and more, there will come a time when He will speak to us! The Holy Ghost is a person, one of the persons of the Godhead. And He speaks:

"As they ministered to the LORD, and fasted, the Holy Ghost said, Separate me Barnabas and Saul for the work whereunto I have called them." (Acts 13:2)

"He that hath an ear, let him hear what the Spirit saith unto the churches; To him that overcometh will I give to eat of the tree of life, which is in the midst of the paradise of God." (Rev. 2:7)

When I first received the infilling of the Holy Ghost I would pray in tongues for more than an hour at a time. While doing this, my first experiences with hearing the voice of God happened this way:

I would pray in tongues, and after a while, the tongues would change into English. And in that English God would tell me something.

Other times, I would pray in tongues for a while. Then I would ask God a question, and then go back to the tongues. As I continued to pray in tongues, the tongues would then change to English and God would give me the answer in the English. As time went on, I would then begin to hear God's voice on the inside of my spirit. And currently this is the main way God speaks to me.

What is hearing God's voice like? Elijah experienced it as a still small voice.

"And after the earthquake a fire; but the LORD was not in the fire: and after the fire a still small voice." (1 Kgs. 19:12)

The best way I can describe **it is that it is like a thought that comes to you, a strong thought**. You may be thinking in your normal way, but then all of a sudden a thought flashes into you. It manifests a little differently from the regular thoughts of your mind. It stands out more. As you begin to be able to concentrate on God more, and focus on Him more, and pray more, you will no doubt begin to experience His still small voice.

This is the wonder of God: that in that special way of praying in tongues, God, through His Spirit, speaks up for us (intercedes), and then also speaks to us.

REVIEW & EXERCISE

Chapter 12:

Q1: Have you ever interpreted your own tongues before?

Q2: What is hearing God's voice like?

Exercise: Pray and ask the Holy Ghost to help you interpret tongues and see what He shows you.

13. SPEAK GOD'S WILL INTO YOUR LIFE

God moves by His Word. He does things by speaking His Word. When He created the world He did it by speaking the Word. He said, "Let there be light," and there was light.

"(As it is written, I have made thee a father of many nations,) before him whom he believed, even God, who quickeneth the dead, and calleth those things which be not as though they were." (Rom. 4:17)

God has plans for our lives. He has ordained many wonderful things for us to accomplish in the future. But although He has ordained these things, for them to actually take place we must birth them into existence. If we look at ourselves, though, the way we are now, we could never achieve these things. They are too mighty for us to accomplish. They could never be for us. But we serve a God that calls those things that be not as though they were. We can allow God to do this for us as we pray in tongues. The Holy Ghost speaks these things into our lives—He actually imprints them into our existence.

For the sake of illustration, let us suppose God calls Brother Jim to be an evangelist. Before Jim moves into that calling he meets much difficulty. He might react negatively. He says to himself: *"I'll never get to be an evangelist. Everything's stacked against me. I don't even have any ability."* And so, because of the discouragement, his spirit is broken. He stops putting forth much effort to move into that calling. He gets lax in his prayer life. He does not read the Bible much anymore. And the result is that he winds up never achieving that call.

On the other hand, if he prays much in tongues, the Holy Ghost, in those tongues, can speak into his spirit, *"Brother Jim will be an evangelist. Brother Jim will be an evangelist. Brother Jim will be an evangelist. Brother Jim will be an evangelist."* Through the speaking in tongues, the Holy Ghost is actually speaking this call into his life, or rather commanding this call to be actualized in his life.

"As the dew of Hermon, and as the dew that descended upon the mountains of Zion: for there the LORD commanded the blessing, even life for evermore." (Ps. 133:3)

"Let them praise the name of the LORD: for he commanded, and they were created." (Ps. 148:5)

"The LORD shall command the blessing upon thee in thy storehouses, and in all that thou settest thine hand unto; and he shall bless thee

in the land which the LORD thy God giveth thee." (Deu. 28:8)

When the Lord speaks the Word of commandment, things happen! As Jim continues to praise in this way, events will change in his life to encourage him, doors will open, his anointing will increase, and he will see signs of his destiny coming to pass.

This is one of the great mysteries of praying in tongues. Things in the natural may not be going our way, but when we pray in tongues the Holy Ghost, in those tongues commands the situation to line up with God's will to bless us.

When God first calls Jim, it seems like there are overwhelming obstacles to Jim, obstacles that are impossible for him to overcome. But as he keeps praying in tongues, the Holy Ghost is calling those things that are not as though they already were. Furthermore, the Holy Ghost, when He speaks, *"Brother Jim will be an evangelist,"* is speaking this also to Jim's spirit. The Holy Ghost communicates messages and impressions to our spirit, most often bypassing the mind: from Spirit to our spirit. The human mind does not have to understand what the Spirit is saying in order to receive from the Spirit. When we allow the Holy Spirit to speak, in tongues, to our spirit, our spirit will receive the message. When that message is firmly rooted in our spirit, then our spirit will deliver that message up to our mind. The understanding of the mind is usually the last step in the Spirit's communication with us. Most people try to understand spiritual things first with their mind, giving rise to intellectualism.

As this message that Jim will be an evangelist is driven into his spirit, his faith will increase, and less and less will he doubt God's call for his life (Jude 20). This message is being "programmed" into Jim by the Holy Ghost. The more he hears it in his inner spirit the more he believes it. The more he believes it the more he acts accordingly and does things that will fulfill this call. The Holy Ghost speaks faith into our life by impressing his messages onto our spirit. And the more we speak in tongues the more we are allowing the Holy Ghost to speak God's will, or His destiny for us, into our lives.

REVIEW & EXERCISE

Chapter 13:

Q1: Name a time in your life where you felt God speak so clearly to you about direction but it felt impossible to achieve.

Q2: What are some unanswered prayers you are still waiting for God to fulfill?

Exercise: Try to pray in tongues and focus on something specific God has promised you.

14. COMMANDING TONGUES

Let us now look at what I call "Commanding Tongues." The Bible tells us that God commands blessings. He can commands certain circumstances or events to become a blessing to us.

"As the dew of Hermon, and as the dew that descended upon the mountains of Zion: for there the LORD commanded the blessing, even life for evermore." (Ps. 133:3)

One time there was a lady who had been looking for a job for several years and did not find any. She then came and joined our church. I was concerned about her situation. One Sunday before I could start preaching, the Spirit led me right up to her seat. In fact, it felt like the Holy Ghost was pushing right up to her. I looked at her and started praying strong tongues as I was in the grip of the Spirit. I kept praying in strong tongues for a while until finally the Spirit lifted and I was able to go back to the pulpit and start the sermon.

About two weeks later she came to church and testified that she had landed a job! At that point the Holy Spirit revealed to me that when I had prayed those strong tongues over her, those were Commanding Tongues which commanded the circumstances in her life to line up with the will of God and bless her with a job!

In the Bible we see God commanded the ravens to bring food to Elijah. Then God commanded the widow to feed Elijah. Jesus commanded the storm to be still. Thus we see God can command situations and events to line up with His will for our blessing. **As we pray much in tongues we will allow the Holy Ghost to operate in Commanding Tongues to command events to line up with God's will and open doors of blessing** which had previously been closed.

REVIEW & EXERCISE

Chapter 14:

Q1: What are "Commanding Tongues?"

Q2: What areas of your life have you prayed with Commanding Tongues and seen fruit produced?

Exercise: Pray in tongues while commanding a stubborn situation to change.

15. GUIDANCE: LED BY THE SPIRIT

"Howbeit when he, the Spirit of truth, is come, he will guide you into all truth: for he shall not speak of himself; but whatsoever he shall hear, that shall he speak: and he will shew you things to come." (Jn. 16:13)

"For as many as are led by the Spirit of God, they are the sons of God." (Rom. 8:14)

One time there was a young man, "Brother J," a former gang member, who got saved and filled with the Holy Ghost gloriously. He got on fire for God and loved to pray in tongues. He needed a job, so he petitioned God and prayed fervently in tongues, and believed God. Then he proceeded to go to a certain place one day to apply for the job. However, when he got there he found out they did not need any more people. He was very disappointed so he started to stroll down another block. As he turned the corner Brother J saw a man in front of the warehouse and started chatting with him. It turned out the man was the boss of a company and desperately needed help. He hired Brother J right on the spot!

So here we see the Holy Ghost functioning as a Guide. Because Brother J was full of the Holy

Ghost, he was sensitive to the leading of the Spirit. It was the Holy Ghost that led him down that street to the warehouse to get a job.

As you discipline your prayer-life to pray more and more in the Spirit, you will become more and more sensitive to the Holy Ghost. You will begin to experience what is known as "being led by the Spirit." The more you are "led by the Spirit" the more you will be led into blessings. Many times Christians use their flesh to try to get a blessing, but then they fail and get disappointed with God. But if they would pray more in the Spirit the Holy Ghost would lead them to blessings they could not even imagine.

REVIEW & EXERCISE

Chapter 15:

Q1: What does it mean to be "led by the Spirit"?

Q2: Was there a time in your life where you felt led by the Spirit?

Exercise: Position yourself to be led by the Spirit and see what He leads you to do.

16. WORSHIP

"But the hour cometh, and now is, when the **true worshippers shall worship the Father in spirit and in truth**: for the Father seeketh such to worship him. God is a Spirit: and they that worship him must worship him in spirit and in truth." (Jn. 4:23-24)

"Cretes and Arabians, we do hear them speak in our tongues the wonderful works of God." (Acts 2:11)

The Holy Ghost accompanies us in our praise and worship of the Lord. On the day of Pentecost, at one point the disciples, in those tongues, were speaking about the wonderful works of God. In other words, the Holy Ghost was praising God through their lips. Those tongues were tongues of praise.

As we spend more time in the Spirit we can move from praise to worship: from tongues of praise to tongues of worship. Many times when I am praising God in tongues the anointing to sing in tongues will come on me. As I get into this, I begin to hear, inside my spirit, certain tunes. What I hear with my spirit, I begin to follow—I go with the flow. I start singing out what I hear. As I do this, my spirit goes higher and higher. Then I sense a heavenly presence, an angelic presence coming on me. What is happening is that I am hearing the angelic choir; and as I respond, my worship attracts the worship angels. They join me in my worship. This edifying, uplifting experience comes from spending much time in the Spirit. And it is the kind of worship that God desires all of his people to have.

The heavenly Father desires for us to worship Him in Spirit and truth. What is "truth?"

"Sanctify them through thy truth: thy word is truth." (Jn. 17:17)

So we see that the Word of God is truth. Most Christians will worship God by using scriptures (the Word) as the basis of their worship and praying in their natural language. This is good, but this only fulfills one part of what God desires. What about worshiping God in Spirit? To do this requires spending time in the Spirit and becoming familiar with the leading of the Spirit, and becoming sensitive to the impressions and touches of the Spirit. As you pray more in more in tongues you will begin to experience this. When you reach the level where you can sing in tongues, sing in heavenly tunes, and sing with angels this will be like a heaven on earth experience!

REVIEW & EXERCISE

Chapter 16:

Q1: What does it mean to worship God in spirit?

Q2: What does it mean to worship God in truth?

Exercise: Try to praise God in tongues until it changes to worship.

17. WARFARE

"Verily I say unto you, Whatsoever ye shall bind on earth shall be bound in heaven: and whatsoever ye shall loose on earth shall be loosed in heaven." (Mat. 18:18)

In Matthew 18:18, we see that Jesus said we had the privilege to bind spirits; whatever we bind will be bound up. If this is the case, why is it that many times the people of God, when the devil is afflicting them, do the binding prayers and plead the blood of Jesus but nothing stops the enemy's attack? To find the answer to this question, go to Acts 13. Here we see the story of a witchdoctor hindering Paul from preaching to the governor of an island. But then Paul, filled with the Holy Spirit, rebuked the witchdoctor, calling blindness on him, and immediately he became blind.

"Then Saul, (who also is called Paul,) filled with the Holy Ghost, set his eyes on him." (Acts 13:9)

This important factor of being filled with the Holy Ghost is often neglected by the saints. Ephesians 5:18 tells us to be filled with the Spirit. Many times Christians are attacked by the enemy. But when they try to rebuke this attack, they are flat in the Spirit—not at all filled with the Spirit. There is no power in their prayer. Recall that in Acts 19, the seven sons of Sceva tried to cast out a devil, but instead, the devil jumped on them. Why? Because they did not have the power of the Spirit. The devil respected Jesus and Paul but not the seven sons of Sceva. The enemy knows who has the power of the Spirit and who does not. So let's make it our business to always be filled with the Holy Spirit. Pray much every day in tongues.

"And be not drunk with wine, wherein is excess; but be filled with the Spirit." (Eph. 5:18)

For a more complete teaching on Warfare see the book: "Warfare that Works."

REVIEW & EXERCISE

Chapter 17:

Q1: Why do binding prayers against the enemy sometimes not work?

Q2: Why does pleading the blood of Christ sometimes not work?

Exercise: Try praying in tongues until you feel full of the Spirit, then bind and plead and see if there is a difference.

18. DISCERNMENT AND TRUTH

"Even the Spirit of truth; whom the world cannot receive, because it seeth him not, neither knoweth him: but ye know him; for he dwelleth with you, and shall be in you." (Jn. 14:17)

"But when the Comforter is come, whom I will send unto you from the Father, even the Spirit of truth, which proceedeth from the Father, he shall testify of me." (Jn. 15:26)

"Howbeit when he, the Spirit of truth, is come, he will guide you into all truth: for he shall not speak of himself; but whatsoever he shall hear, that shall he speak: and he will shew you things to come." (Jn. 16:13)

"We are of God: he that knoweth God heareth us; he that is not of God heareth not us. Hereby know we the spirit of truth, and the spirit of error." (1 Jn. 4:6)

Jesus many times called the Holy Ghost the Spirit of Truth. **The more we pray in the Holy Ghost the sharper our discernment of the Truth becomes.** We do not want to be deceived. The enemy loves to deceive us, and rightly he is labeled the father of lies. When we get deceived we go astray and miss many, many blessings and suffer disappointment and heartache. But the more we pray in the Holy Ghost the more the Spirit of Truth can operate in our lives.

Once, when I began pastoring, a young lady came to me for counseling. She asked me to pray for her mother because the mother was "filled with the devil" and was always yelling at the daughter with a "sharp tongue." So I prayed for this situation as she had requested, and then went into tongues. As I was praying in tongues all of a sudden, I burst forth and said to the girl, *"You have a sharp tongue. You yourself talk rough to your mother."* She got indignant and vehemently denied it.

As the days went on I started looking at her more carefully. And sure enough, when she did not think I was looking, she would talk badly to people. I began to see this more and more. The Holy Ghost certainly was the Spirit of Truth. So often we are fooled by people. One of the most common ways saints get hurt is when they believe things people tell them. As a result, we become deceived and taken advantage of. But if we pray more and more in the Holy Ghost, the Holy Ghost will operate as the Spirit of Truth in our lives and our discernment of the Truth will get sharper and sharper.

REVIEW & EXERCISE

Chapter 18:

Q1: Why is the Holy Ghost known as the Spirit of Truth?

Q2: Why is it crucial to have the Spirit of Truth in our lives?

Exercise: While praying in tongues, ask the Holy Spirit to reveal truth so you can bind the lies of the enemy.

19. BIRTHING BY THE SPIRIT

The day after receiving the baptism of the Holy Ghost in 1974, I was in the church prayer room praying in tongues for about an hour when I got a vision of a multitude of poor Chinese people with their hands raised. They were reaching for the good things the communist government had promised them. Of course they got nothing, but they were so desperate that they kept their hands raised hoping and waiting for anyone, anywhere to give them something good. Then I heard the Lord say to me that He was going to raise me up as a minister and send me to China one day to preach. My reaction was, "No, I don't want to go to China."

I had hated communism for the misery it had caused my parents (who were fortunate enough to escape to America) and did not want anything to do with communist China. As I kept praying in tongues this vision would not leave me. I wished that it would go away but it didn't. "I do not want to go there," I kept telling the Lord.

And then something happened. I began to feel sorry for the people. And then I realized it was really Jesus that the people were reaching out for. By the end of the second hour of prayer I was weeping for the people.

As the third hour of prayer progressed I began to feel the sorrow for the people in my stomach. After a while I felt a wrenching in my stomach, like I was having a baby, and I feel to the floor, weeping and agonizing profusely. It seemed like it would never end. Finally, after five hours of intense prayer, the Spirit lifted from me and I could rest.

This event happened in 1974 at the height of the Cold War between the USA and China. No Americans were allowed to visit China then, and the leaders of China had wiped out all religion. So some Christians told me my vision was impossible.

Some years later, the doors to China opened and I was invited to conduct a conference in the middle of China for underground pastors who were hungry for the Holy Ghost. On the last day of the meeting, the Holy Ghost swept into the barn where we were and all the pastors' hands shot up as Holy fire ignited everyone and they were baptized in the Spirit and started speaking in tongues. The vision that I had years ago now manifested.

Looking back on that day I had the vision, I now realize that God had put me into travailing prayer till I became pregnant with the burden of China and then finally birthed the China ministry. My China destiny had become ordained in heaven and nothing could abort it until the day it manifested physically here on earth.

Many saints receive prophecies of wonderful destinies, but all too often these prophecies never come to pass. One reason is that the people just think all they have to do is believe and receive and everything will come to pass. But more than faith is required; birthing is required! Whatever vision, dream or destiny you believe God has promised you, start praying in tongues, and fervently keep pressing in deeper and deeper till you become pregnant with it. The tongues you are speaking will take on a new force. As the hours and days pass, the "burden" of that vision will get stronger and stronger till at last it is birthed.

Don't give up. **Learn to pray strong and long in tongues and many wonderful promises will be birthed in your life!**

REVIEW & EXERCISE

Chapter 19:

Q1: What is "Birthing by the Spirit?"

Q2: Why do so many prophecies and visions go unfulfilled?

Exercise: When a heavy burden comes upon you, try praying until it lifts

20. TRUTH VS. MISCONCEPTIONS ABOUT TONGUES

Basically there are two purposes for tongues:

1) Personal edification. (1Cor. 14:14)

2) Giving a message or prophecy to the congregation or a body of believers. (1 Cor. 14:26-28).

For the first (personal edification), no interpretation is needed. The great apostle Paul himself said that when he prayed in tongues his understanding was unfruitful (1 Cor. 14.14)

For the second purpose, when we are among a body of believers, and someone bursts forth in tongues, there should be interpretation. Those tongues should bring forth a message or prophecy for the group. One time I was at a church, and a Pastor Wallace was about to preach. A lady then stood up and broke forth in tongues. Then she sat down with no interpretation being done. The next day the same thing happened— the lady spoke out in tongues but no interpretation after that. The third day, as Pastor Wallace was starting to preach, the same lady got up and burst forth again in tongues. This time Pastor Wallace told her to sit down, telling her, "If you can't bring forth the interpretation for your tongues, just sit down and don't interrupt the service."

Of course, there are times the pastor may want the whole congregation to start speaking in tongues to build up the anointing in the service because the spiritual atmosphere had been flat. In this case, no interpretation is necessary because we are praying in tongues for edification. You may say, *"Why doesn't God let us understand all our tongues?"* Because the Holy Ghost makes intercession for us (Rom. 8.26) and many times He is praying to avert some danger the enemy has planned for you. If you knew what the Holy Ghost was saying, you might become fearful and think, "The devil is going to try to kill me today. Oh my, I better stay home under the covers."

"For he that speaketh in an unknown tongue speaketh not unto men, but unto God: for no man understandeth him; howbeit in the spirit he speaketh mysteries." (1 Cor. 14:2)

"For if I pray in an unknown tongue, my spirit prayeth, but my understanding is unfruitful. *What is it then? I will pray with the spirit, and I will pray with the understanding also: I will sing with the spirit, and I will sing with the understanding also." (1 Cor. 14:14-15)*

"How is it then, brethren? when ye come together, every one of you hath a psalm, hath a doctrine, hath a tongue, hath a revelation, hath an interpretation. Let all things be done unto edifying. If any man speak in an unknown tongue, let it be by two, or at the most by three, and that by course; and let one interpret. But if there be no interpreter, let him keep silence in the church; and let him speak to himself, and to God." (1 Cor. 14:26-28)

"Likewise the Spirit also helpeth our infirmities: for we know not what we should pray for as we ought: but the Spirit itself maketh intercession for us with groanings which cannot be uttered." (Rom. 8:26)

REVIEW & EXERCISE

Chapter 20:

Q1: What are the two purposes of tongues?

Q2: When is no interpretation necessary for tongues?

Exercise: In a small group setting, have one person pray in tongues while another attempts to interpret and see what happens!

21. CONCLUSION

Jesus felt that the least His disciples could pray was one hour.

"And he cometh unto the disciples, and findeth them asleep, and saith unto Peter, What, could ye not watch with me one hour?" (Mat. 26:40)

If we want to be worthy servants of the Lord this is the least we can do. If we want to be strong in the Lord, this is the least we can do.

"Finally, my brethren, be strong in the LORD, and in the power of his might." (Eph. 6:10)

A good habit would be to pray an hour everyday: half the time in our normal language, and half the time in tongues!

Remember this:

Much prayer, much power.
Some prayer, some power,
Little prayer, little power.
No prayer, no power.

EXERCISE

Chapter 21:

Exercise 1: Pray in the natural for a half an hour.

Exercise 2: Pray in tongues for a half an hour.

POWER SECRETS REVEALED

Today more than ever before the modern church needs power from on high. The pressures of living in these end times has almost reached a boiling point. Being *stressed out* seems to be the normal mode for people, even longtime Christians. In this book, Donald Lee shows how to take dominion over these forces that are coming against us. Secrets of the power of praying in tongues are revealed and clearly explained here. Some of the things you will learn:

- **Changing your future**
- **Tongues that command circumstances**
- **Warfare Tongues**
- **Tongues that comfort and break discouragement**
- **Getting gifts of the Holy Spirit**
- **Experience the tangible presence of God**
- **Hearing God's voice**

As you apply these simple principles, your life will be dramatically empowered and revolutionized.

* * * * * * * * *

Donald Lee was supernaturally called by God into the Ministry of the Apostle. In 1975, while evangelizing, the finger of God physically appeared and wrote the word "Apostle" on his forehead. Anointed and equipped with the gifts of the Holy Spirit, Reverend Lee and his teams have brought the good news of the Gospel to more than 80 nations: from Asia to Australia, from the Orient to North, Central and South America, and from Europe to Africa.

He also served for 25 years as an educator, specializing in learning theory. His mandate from the Lord is to make saints strong and guide them into their destiny.

For information of other materials, and his mentoring program contact:
Godshealingstream@gmail.com
www.GodsHealingStream.org

God's Healing Stream
P.O. Box 1503
Fort Mill, SC 29716

For a free audio ("pray-along in tongues") send your name and email to:

successwithdonaldlee@gmail.com

Made in the USA
Middletown, DE
30 September 2018